SKATEBOARDING

by
JacksonTeller

CAPSTONE PRESS
a capstone imprint

Velocity is published by
Capstone Press, a Capstone imprint,
151 Good Counsel Drive, P.O. Box 669,
Mankato, Minnesota 56002.

www.capstonepub.com

First published 2011
Copyright © 2011 A & C Black
Publishers Limited

Original concept: Paul Mason
Project management: Paul Mason
Design: Mayer Media

J796.22
TEL

Printed and bound in Malaysia by Tien Wah
Press

032011
006117ACF11

Library of Congress Cataloging-in-Publication
Data

Teller, Jackson.
  Skateboarding : how to be an awesome
skateboarder / by Jackson Teller,
for Mason Media.
     p. cm. -- (Velocity: instant expert)
  Includes index.
  ISBN 978-1-4296-6883-5 (library binding)
  1. Skateboarding--Juvenile literature. 2.
Skateboarders--Juvenile
literature. I. Title. II. Series.
  GV859.8.T45 2012
  796.22--dc22
                              2011010224

WARNING!
Some of the techniques described in
this book are dangerous, or can lead
to dangerous situations if performed
incorrectly. Only undertake them when you
are 100% confident you can do so safely.

This book is produced using paper made from
wood grown in managed, sustainable forests.
It is natural, renewable, and recyclable. The
logging and manufacturing processes conform
to the environmental regulations of the
country of origin.

Picture acknowledgements
Grateful thanks to all those whose images
made this book possible:
Tinou Bao 11 (top left); Michele Bartoletti
Stella 35 (bottom); 39 Jeff Cadge (top right);
25 Robert Cianflone; Lewis Collins 5, 7 (right
top and bottom), 8 (top), 9, 12 (middle and
bottom), 13 (bottom left, right top and bottom),
14, 15, 16, 17, 18, 19, 20, 21, 22, 23 (left top and
bottom), 26, 27 (bottom left and right), 29
(right top and bottom), 30-31 ollie sequence,
32, 33, 34-35 dropping in sequence, 36, 37
(top, right top and bottom), 38, 39 (right top
and bottom), 42 (bottom left and right, 43
(right); Getty Images 24, 25 (main); William
Hoiles 31 top; 43 Dex Image (top and bottom
right); Imagr8mom 10 (bottom); 1, 44 Heath
Korvola; Jamie Lantzy 5; Charles Lillo 10
(inset); Joe Mabel 36-7 (centre), 39; Dom
Mason 10 (top), 11 (bottom); Paul Mason 7 (left
top and bottom), 23 (right), 27 (top left and
right), 28, 29 left (top and bottom), 40, 41,
42 (top); Andrew Parodi 4; Aaron Pruzaniec
11 (bottom right); 39, 47 Jay Reilly (bottom
right); Chad Santos 25 (inset); Lewis Sharman
31 (top, inset); Surrey Skateboards 12 (top), 13
(top left); Felipe Vaiano 8 (bottom).

Cover photos: Shutterstock; Heath Korvola
(bottom, left centre)

Where appropriate, every effort has been
made to contact copyright holders of material
reproduced in this book. Any omissions will
be rectified in subsequent editions if the
publisher is given notice.

Contents

Why become a
skateboard expert?

Ever ridden along with the wheels on your deck shaking your feet like a rollercoaster? Or found yourself lying on the sidewalk, wondering why you suddenly stopped rolling – only to see that one of your trucks has come off? Or just wanted to know how to build up your dream deck from scratch? Then this book is for you.

HELP YOUR FRIENDS
Not only will you find out how to get *your* skateboard rolling as sweetly as a marble across a pool table. You'll also be able to step in *just* as your friends are about to give up, point out exactly what they're doing wrong, and show them how to put the problem right. How satisfying is that?

SAVE CASH!
Every time you go into a skate store to get something changed or fixed, it costs money. With a few simple tools, most jobs can be done at home - saving you lots of cash to spend on new skate gear.

FYI!
These features are scattered throughout the book. They contain information you can casually drop into conversation to amaze, astound, and impress your friends.

Whatever kind of skating you (or your friends) do, you can probably do it better using the tips in this book.

SPECIAL TOOLS
The tools you need for most jobs are listed on page 9. Some jobs require a specialist kit, which is listed in panels like this one.

LOST FOR WORDS
Look here for explanations of those tricky, technical words.

FINDING THE RIGHT INFO
Whatever kind of skating you are into, you will find this book crammed with helpful information. From how to personalize your **grip tape** design to servicing your **bearings**, recognizing different tricks, doing an ollie properly, and the rules of behavior in the skate park, you'll find plenty of useful information. You'll even get to know the ins and outs of skateboarding's special language, and drop words like 'stalefish' and 'method' into the conversation.

Types of skateboards

There used to be one basic type of skateboard, but today there are many. The basic types are standard skateboards and longboards. Standard boards are used for modern aggressive skating: ramp riding, tricks on the street, and flatland skills. Longer boards are used for cruising around, riding in a more relaxed way.

If you're picking a board, the biggest choice is probably between wheels:
• **Soft wheels are good for cruising around.**
• **Hard wheels are used for tricks and ramps.**

DECK SHAPE
The deck is the part of the board your feet feel most directly. Its shape has an important effect on how the board rides. Most decks have a raised tail, nose and sides, which together are called the **concave**. Deeper concaves allow skaters to perform more aggressive tricks. Shallower concaves are easier for inexperienced skaters to use.

STANDARD SKATEBOARDS
Standard skateboards are usually about 76cm/30in long, and about 20cm/8in wide. These boards are used for the kinds of skateboarding that are most popular today:
• Street skating, which features technical jumps, spins, flips and slides using features such as handrails, concrete blocks and curbs
• Ramp skating, on everything from small mini-ramps to giant mega-ramps
• Flatland, where skaters pull off some amazing aerials and spins from (you guessed it) flat land

concave amount of lift in the nose, tail and sides of a skateboard deck

manual trick where the skater rides along balancing on only the back wheels

TOP TIP
Skateboards are pretty simple devices. It's the combination of different types of deck, wheel, truck and other parts that make them complicated.

This shot shows the wheels and concave most clearly, as well as the flip at the nose and tail of the board.

LONGBOARD SKATEBOARDS
Any board over 89cm/35in long is generally thought of as a longboard. Longboards are mainly used for cruising around in a relaxed style. They are too big and heavy for modern skate tricks. Some skaters like to do tricks like **manuals**, cross-stepping, and tail slides on a longboard. Shorter, looser longboard-style decks are used for slalom. Longer, stiffer boards are used for downhill racing.

From below you can see the trucks and deck shape. Note the width of the trucks compared to the deck – neither too wide or too narrow.

FYI!
Manufacturers have developed an off-road skateboard called a mountain board. Just put your feet in the straps and roll downhill!

Basic **equipment**

Skateboarding equipment is pretty much divided between the board (See pages 6 and 7.) and stuff that keeps you safe if you crash. For beginners and vert-ramp riders, it is a good idea to wear as much safety equipment as you can. Other skaters restrict themselves to a helmet.

HELMETS

A helmet is the only piece of equipment a skater really has to own (apart from a skateboard – definitely buy that first). Many skate parks will not let you ride unless you are wearing one. Even if you are allowed to ride without one, helmets make sense. Broken wrists heal, but a broken head may not. It's worth checking that a helmet is **hallmarked** with your country's safety-approval mark, which proves it will work in an accident.

PADS

Few experienced skateboarders wear pads, which is a shame: pads are great at preventing injuries! It is easier to learn new tricks wearing a helmet and pads because you're less nervous about falling when you know it probably won't hurt. As with helmets, check that pads are hallmarked with a safety-approval mark.

hallmarked mark showing that goods meet safety standards
vert ramp double-sided ramp with walls that end up vertical

As well as a board, helmet and pads, some riders use:
- **specialist backpack, with external straps to carry the board too**

BASIC TOOLS

Only very basic tools are needed for working on a skateboard. Most skaters manage with a specialist skate tool. These combine a socket to fit truck bolts of the size usually found on skateboards, a screwdriver, and two different spanners. With these almost every job can be done, but a flathead screwdriver and a small adjustable wrench also come in handy.

FYI!

Some early skateboards had rattly metal wheels. Modern skateboard wheels were invented in 1972 by Frank Nasworthy.

SECRET TRICK

It is never a good idea to borrow or buy a helmet that doesn't fit properly. In a crash, it will come off or slide around, which makes wearing it pointless.

1 Check the basic fit by pulling one strap then the other. The helmet needs to be snug enough not to move.

2 The forehead gets uncomfortable very quickly if the helmet is too tight.

3 The straps need to be done up and fit snugly under the chin. Leave a small gap, though – too tight and you won't be able to breathe properly!

From **sidewalk surfer** to **skater**

Skateboarding first appeared in the 1950s, though skating as we know it developed in the 1970s. Although its popularity has always gone in and out of fashion, there has always been a hard core of dedicated skaters, and this core is getting bigger and bigger.

THE SIDEWALK SURFERS

The first skateboarders appeared some time in the 1950s – no one recorded the exact first time. They were surfers who wanted something to do when the waves went flat, or they couldn't get to the beach. They nailed roller skate trucks to the bottom of old planks of wood and used them to scoot around on the sidewalk. They soon became known as sidewalk surfers.

1970s SKATE REVOLUTION

In the mid-1970s, there was a revolution in skateboarding. Out went the old surfing-influenced moves, and in came an aggressive new form of skating. The revolution began in drained swimming pools in California. Skaters used the sides and lips of the pools to launch aerials and perform tricks. Then, in 1978, a Florida skater named 'Ollie' Gelfand invented the most important trick in modern skating: the **ollie**.

ollie when a skater jumps the board into the air using only his/her feet

TONY HAWK RESCUES SKATING

During the 1980s, the popularity of skateboarding crashed. Many skate parks closed – the sport was seen as dangerous, and the parks could not get insurance against skaters being injured. One skater dragged skateboarding back to popularity almost single-handedly. His name was Tony Hawk. Hawk's radical vert-ramp riding inspired a new generation of skaters. After the release of his Pro Skater computer game in 1999, the sport became even more popular.

SECRET HISTORY

At times, skateboarding has been seen as so dangerous that it should be banned! Of course, this only made skating more popular among its young, rebellious fans.

The most famous ban was in Norway, where it was not allowed for 11 years between 1978 and 1989. Skaters built secret ramps deep in the Norwegian woods, and snuck off there to practice without the interference of the police.

FYI!

Skateboards are not just fun – they are useful for getting around on. Even the U.S. Marine Corps has experimented with using skateboards for transportation.

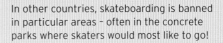

NO BIKING SKATING SKATEBOARDING

In other countries, skateboarding is banned in particular areas – often in the concrete parks where skaters would most like to go!

One man and his skateboard collection. This is what happens when you never get rid of old boards!

Designing **your own board**

Lots of people buy their skateboards assembled, which is good value for money. But many expert skaters prefer to design their own board. They pick the deck, wheels, trucks, bearings and other components they think will suit them best. Designing your own skateboard in this way is very satisfying.

The special tools you need for designing your own board are in your head:
- **A clear idea of what kind of skating you plan to do**
- **A bit of imagination**

TRUCKS AND BUSHINGS

In general, narrower trucks are more moveable, and wider ones are more stable. Trucks should be more-or-less as wide as the deck. On a standard board they are usually about 20cm/8in wide. On a longboard, the trucks are wider, up to 23cm/9in or more. The truck bushings come in varying degrees of softness.

DECKS

Most skateboard decks are made of wood, often **7-ply**. Standard decks are usually about 76cm/30in long, and about 20cm/8in wide. Skaters vary the length and width of their decks depending on things like weight and shoe size. Any board over 89cm/35in long is generally thought of as a longboard. Many longboards are a lot bigger than this at 102cm/40in or more.

GRIP TAPE

Grip tape for the deck of the board is an unglamorous but crucial weapon in a skater's armory. Almost all tricks, including just standing on the board without sliding off, would be impossible without it.

7-ply wood made out of seven thin layers glued together
ABEC measurement of the quality of ball bearings
durometer rating number showing the hardness of a skateboard wheel

WHEELS
Wheels make a BIG difference to how a skateboard rides. On a standard deck, the wheels are normally about 56mm/2.2in in diameter, and have a **durometer rating** of 90a or greater. Longboard wheels like those in the photo are bigger and softer than a standard skateboard's, with sizes over 60mm/2.4in and durometer ratings of less than 90a.

BEARINGS
Bearings are available in various grades, from **ABEC** 1 to ABEC 9. Skaters get very concerned about bearing quality, and many people spend extra money on bearings with a high ABEC number. In fact, though, ABEC 1 bearings are good enough for all skate uses.

SECRET TRICK
Experienced skaters know what width of deck they like. But how does everyone else work out how wide their deck should be?

For bigger feet, a deck over 20cm/8in wide will usually feel best. For smaller feet, a narrower deck will be easier to move.

Type of skating also affects deck width. Go a little wider for ramps and cruising around, and go narrower for street skating.

FYI!
One of the most popular woods for decks is Canadian maple. Some manufacturers have also started using bamboo, which is said to be better for the environment.

13

Changing **truck bushings**

No special tools are needed for this job. You may find it easier if you remove the trucks from the deck first, though (see pages 16 and 17).

Truck bushings really affect how a skateboard rides. Soft bushings allow the board to lean more and make it turn well, but it's harder to land tricks because the board is wobbly. Stiffer bushings give more control, but turn less easily. Bushings need to be changed when they wear out, and also if you want to alter the way your board rides.

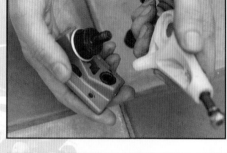

STRIP DOWN, CLEAN AND REPLACE

Continue taking the parts of the truck off the kingpin and laying them out in order. The only tricky part is sometimes the **hanger**, the wide metal part that the wheels bolt on to. Pull this from its socket and slide it up the kingpin. Underneath you will find a second, larger bushing and washer. Slide these off too. Now clean everything and check it for damage to see if any parts need to be replaced.

REMOVE THE KINGPIN NUT

The kingpin is the large bolt that runs through the middle of the trucks. A skate tool will fit almost all kingpin nuts. Loosen this and then pull it out. At the same time, pull off the washer underneath the nut, then the top bushing. Lay the parts out on an old sheet of newspaper in order as you take them off.

hanger wide, metal part of a truck, on to which the wheels are bolted

spacer piece of plastic fitted between skateboard trucks and the deck

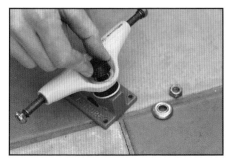

REASSEMBLE WITH NEW BUSHINGS

All your parts should be laid out in order, so just take the old bushings out of the line and replace them with the new ones. Then push everything back on to the kingpin in order, and tighten the kingpin nut. How tightly this is done up will affect how soft your trucks feel. Looser will be better for a carvey, turny setup. Tighter will be better for tricks, as it makes the trucks more stable when you land.

SECRET TRICK

If you put softer bushings into your trucks, you will probably need to add a **spacer** to each truck:

Without spacers, the extra lean from the soft bushings causes the wheels to rub against the bottom of the deck.

Adding spacers means the wheels can spin freely, even at a full lean angle.

FYI!

Sometimes you can wring a bit of extra life out of your bushings by turning the large one (the one nearest the deck) over and putting it on the other way around.

Truck removal and **installation**

Skateboard trucks are pretty tough – but it is possible to break them or wear them out! If that happens, you'll need to replace them. But most skaters only remove trucks when they buy a new deck. In these photos, we're changing the trucks from an old deck to a new one.

REMOVING THE TRUCKS
Each truck is held in place by four flat-headed screws. With the deck resting on its side, hold a screw head in place using a screwdriver or allen key, depending on which your trucks use. From underneath the deck, loosen the nut on that same screw. Repeat for the other three trucks, and you should be able to lift the trucks free from the deck.

FYI!
Truck sizes are measured two ways: by the width of the axle (which should be close to the width of the deck) or by the size of the hanger.

INSTALL SCREWS ON NEW DECK
Once the trucks are off, remove the screws from the old deck. These can be stubborn and tough to shift. If so, check out the Secret Trick on the right. Replace any that are bent, then push them up through the truck-screw holes in the new deck.

FASTEN TRUCKS TO DECK

Now put the new trucks in place. Some skaters position the truck over the holes, then push the screws through. It's probably easier to push the screws through, then slide the truck over them. Using your fingers, tighten the nuts onto all four screws as far as possible. Finally, tighten them snugly using a skate tool or spanner – don't forget to hold the screw head in place as you do this, or the screw will just turn without tightening!

Phillips-head screwdriver with a narrow, four-pointed-star tip

SECRET TRICK

Removing truck screws from an old deck can be a tricky job. Here are a couple of easy ways to do it:

1 Lay the deck faceup on a hard surface (NOT your parents' favorite kitchen table, desk, etc.). Press down as hard as you can on the nose and tail, and the screws should pop up.

2 Really stubborn screws can be knocked out using the base of the truck you've just removed.

Changing **wheels**

Any skate tool or **socket wrench** can be used to change your wheels.

Wheels wear out, or riders want to change them for harder or softer ones to get a different kind of ride from their board. Removing and working on wheels are quick and easy jobs, but there are one or two tips that not everyone knows, which will make your board run more sweetly.

TAKE OFF THE LOCKNUT
Each wheel is held in place by a locknut, a nut that has a plastic liner on some of its threads. Locknuts get their name from the way the plastic liner stops the nut from coming loose once it has been tightened. The nut is 'locked' in place. At first, locknuts feel a bit stiff. You won't be able to unscrew them by hand, even after freeing them up.

TAKE OFF THE WHEEL
Once the locknut is off, slide everything off the axle. As well as the wheel itself, there may be **washers** on either side of the wheel. Lay these out in the order they come off, so that it's easy to remember how everything goes back together. If you are changing your bearings, this is the moment to take them out of the wheel. See pages 20 and 21 for advice on how to do this.

socket wrench type of spanner that fits over a nut and is used to undo it
washer tiny metal ring that fits either side of a skateboard wheel

1 Tighten the locknut down softly until the wheels fit snugly. Then undo it a quarter turn so that the bearing is very slightly loose.

REPLACE THE WHEELS
Slide the wheels, and everything else, back on to the truck axle the same way it all came off. If you took the wheels off simply to clean or replace the bearings, this will be an easy job. Even if you have replaced the entire wheel, everything should still fit together in the same way, as long as your new wheels are the same width as the old ones. Tighten down the locknut – see the Secret Trick on the right for a tip on how to get the tension just right.

FYI!
Most skaters have their wheel graphics on the outside – but it makes no difference in performance. You can ride them with the graphics inside if you prefer.

2 Check the tension by moving the wheel side to side on the axle. There should be enough movement to make a little clicking noise.

Bearing **removal** and **replacement**

Bearings are the things that make your wheels turn, so they're a pretty important part of the skateboard. If the bearings start to feel gritty or won't roll properly, they may need either cleaning or changing. This feels like a slightly scary job the first time you do it, but take it step by step and it's actually pretty simple.

As well as a skate tool, for cleaning bearings you will also need:
- **spray lubricant**
- **old rags and newspaper**

REMOVING THE BEARINGS
First, remove the wheels (see pages 18 and 19). Now you have two options: take your wheels to a skate store, where they have a special tool for removing bearings, or do it yourself. Doing it yourself is more satisfying. First, lay the board on its deck and kneel or lean on it. Hook the tip of the axle back into the wheel so that it touches the bearing but not the inside of the wheel.

LEVER THE BEARING OUT
Now gently lever down on the axle to start pulling the bearing out of the wheel. You may need to try this at different spots around the bearing to lever it right off. Once the first one is off, remove the second bearing on the other side of the wheel. Take out any **spacers**. Repeat this process on all four wheels.

FYI!
Some pro skaters turn their bearings around so that you can't see what brand they use. It's because they are using bearings by a company that doesn't sponsor them.

bearing shield plastic or rubber cover that protects against water and dirt
spacers pieces of plastic used inside skateboard wheels to keep bearings the correct distance apart

SECRET TRICK

Cleaning bearings may make them last a bit longer. This is a quick way to clean up cheap bearings. (Warning: it's a messy job!)

1 Hold the bearing over an old newspaper or tissue with the **bearing shield** outwards. Spray lubricant into the edges.

FIT NEW BEARINGS

Now you can press your lovely new bearings into place. Don't forget to drop the spacers between the two bearings, if they are needed. Slide the wheels back on to the truck axle, and tighten down the locknut. You may need to use a little extra pressure, because after fitting new bearings the locknut pushes everything firmly together. Set the tension as shown in the Secret Trick on page 19.

2 Loads of black gunk will come out of the bearing and drip onto the paper. Keep spraying lubricant until the fluid that runs out of the bearing is clear.

Installing **grip tape**

Putting the grip tape on a board is a magic moment. It's a statement of intent. Without grip tape, you can't really do more than trundle along a gentle slope. With it, you can do ollies, ride vert, perform power slides, and practice all kinds of other skateboarding techniques.

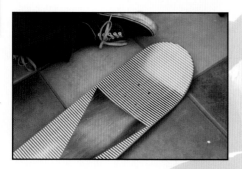

CUT THE TAPE TO SIZE

First, lay the new deck on to a strip of grip tape. Mark a little longer than the board – a hand's width should be plenty – and cut the tape to roughly the correct length.

(NB grip tape is tough, and blunts scissors really quickly – use old ones, not your sister's best sewing scissors!)

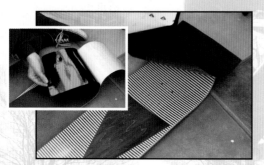

STICK THE TAPE DOWN

Place the tape on the deck to double check that you haven't cut it too short, and that there's enough to take account of the nose and tail kicks. Set the tape aside and use sandpaper to roughen up the deck wherever the tape is going. Peel about 5cm/2in of backing off the tape and stick it to the nose. Slowly peel the rest of the backing off, pressing the tape down on the deck as you go.

TRIM EXCESS TAPE

Rub the edges of the deck with the side of a screwdriver, which will mark the outline of the board. Bend the tape up and down along this line to weaken it along this outline. Now trim along the line with a box cutter – very carefully, because if you slip it's easy to cut yourself. The longer and smoother your cuts, the neater the job will turn out.

You do need some extra tools for this job:
- **box cutter or hobby knife**
- **screwdriver**
- **flat file**
- **pencil**
- **sandpaper**

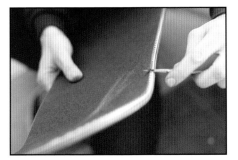

FINAL FINISHING

To get a really good finish, you can trim the edges of the tape with a flat file. (Always file down and away from the deck.) Finally, push holes in the tape where the truck bolts will go through, using a **bradawl** or small allen key.

bradawl tool with a thin, pointed tip that is used to make holes

SECRET TRICK

No one says grip tape has to cover the whole deck!

1 You might at least want to show off the maker's logo in front of the back trucks.

2 Or you might want something completely wild, like discs of grip or some other unusual shape.

FYI!

WATCH OUT! This job requires the use of sharp tools, so ask an adult to help you with this project.

Skate greats

Is it a bird? Is it a plane? No, it's skating superman Danny Way, soaring high above the crowds!

Who are the greatest skaters ever? Get three skaters together, and you can guarantee you'll hear at least three different opinions (plus one of them will probably change his or her mind halfway through). Here's a selection of some of the skateboarders most people consider to be modern skate greats:

TONY HAWK (USA)

Earth's most famous skateboarder? Probably. Tony Hawk is considered by most people to be the best vert-ramp skater in history. His amazingly long career as a pro rider started when he was just 14, and 20 years later in 2002 – at the age of 34 – he was still good enough to win an **X Games** gold medal.

X Games extreme sports competition featuring many skateboarding events

RODNEY MULLEN (USA)

Mullen is probably the most influential skater ever because of the sheer number of tricks he has invented. Rodney is so determined that in 2007, he started teaching himself to skate with his right foot forward instead of his left. His right hip joint had started to wear out.

CHRIS COLE (USA)

The winner of *Thrasher Magazine's* Skater of the Year Award in both 2005 and 2009, Cole is one of the world's top street skaters. He won X Games gold medals in 2006 (for Street) and 2007 (for Street and Best Street Trick).

CHRIS HASLAM (CANADA)

A top goofy-foot skater, Haslam's full-on approach is popular with other skaters. As a result he won the Reader's Choice award at the

Transworld Skateboarding awards in 2005. Haslam also won the Vs 411VM contest in 2006. In this, the public votes on who goes through to the next round of competition, and who finally wins.

DANNY WAY (USA)

Danny started skating when he was 5, and some sources say he won his first contest at the age of 6. As an adult Danny has concentrated on ramp riding, using the biggest ramps to launch the biggest aerials possible. In 2005, for example, he jumped the Great Wall of China on a skateboard.

DAEWON SONG (USA)

Daewon is a legendary street skater and co-star of the movie *Rodney Mullen vs. Daewon Song*, in which the two try to outdo each other. (The two are also co-owners of Almost Skateboards.) Daewon is most famous for his vast array of tricks and his ability to fuse together old-school and modern skating.

Street skating superstar Tony Hawk shows off his incredible vert ramp skills.

Basic **stance** and **moving the board**

One of the things it's crucial to get right is your stance. **Get this right, and the tricks and techniques of modern skating become much easier. Get it wrong, and everything from an ollie on up will become more difficult than it needs to be. Learned in combination with moving the board, a good stance gets you comfortable with a deck under your feet.**

For the Secret Trick, you will find it useful to have:
• **a ball**
• **some stairs**

BASIC STANCE
At first it's best to practice this with the skateboard standing on some grass or an old piece of carpet so that it cannot roll away. Just get used to standing on the board while moving your feet around and balancing on only the front or back wheels. Then get used to moving your back foot into the angle of the rear kicktail and moving your front foot so that it's over the truck bolts.

MOVING THE BOARD
Most skaters ride with their left foot at the front of the board. This is called regular stance. Riding with your right foot forward is known as goofy. Most skaters push off with their back foot, but a few feel more comfortable using their front foot.

Turn your front foot so that it angles toward the nose of the board. Put your back foot down on the ground.

Push off backward with your back foot. It's more important to stay balanced than to give a big push.

SECRET TRICK

When you first start skating, it can be tricky to work out which foot goes at the back of the board. These tricks should help you work it out:

FYI!
Experienced skaters can ride with their front or back foot forward. Riding with your back foot forward is called riding **fakie**.

If you kick a ball with your right foot, that's probably your back foot.

If you use your right foot first when walking upstairs, that's a sign it's your back foot.

FYI!
Always keep your knees bent when skating. It makes everything easier!

As soon as it feels natural, lift your back foot off the ground.

Smoothly transfer your back foot back onto the deck, and roll along until the board starts to slow down. Repeat until you can do this smoothly and without thinking.

 fakie traveling backward on a skateboard **stance** how a skater stands on the board

27

Turning and stopping

Once you're able to get a skateboard moving, the next thing to get comfortable with is turning it so you can steer around obstacles. You should also stop it, in case you spot any obstacles you can't steer around! (Every skater, from beginner to expert, has experienced the need to do an emergency stop because of an unexpected pedestrian.)

TURNING THE BOARD

The easiest way to turn a skateboard is by putting extra weight on one side of the deck. This causes the board to turn to the side you have weighted. Putting weight down on the **toe side** of the deck will steer the board in that direction. Putting weight on the **heel side** will steer the opposite way. All this is much easier, and works better, if you ride with bent knees, crouching loosely over the board.

STARTING TO SLOW DOWN

To slow the board down, you need to use your back foot as a brake. Turn your front foot so that it faces the nose of the board. Put all your weight on your front foot, and place your back foot down flat to the ground. The friction should start to slow the board down.

> **heel side** edge of a skateboard deck to which your heels are closest
> **toe side** edge of a skateboard deck to which your toes are closest

SECRET TRICK

Foot braking is not the only way to stop a skateboard. Here are a couple of others that are harder to learn – and much more spectacular!

1 This skater is using a technique called heel braking. He is basically doing a wheelie and dragging his back foot on the ground.

GETTING THE WEIGHT RIGHT

The idea is to drag the sole of your shoe along the ground like the brake on a bike. If your foot keeps skipping up, you are applying too much pressure. Try again, with a little less weight on your back foot. Keep practicing until you can get the pressure just right every time.

FYI!

Practice braking on a very slight slope with no pedestrians or vehicles around. A slope with a grassy area is ideal in case you don't manage to stop the first few times!

2 This technique is called a power slide. The skater puts extra weight on his front foot and pushes his back foot out like a snowboarder skidding to a stop.

Learning to **ollie**

The ollie first appeared in the late 1970s, when Adam 'Ollie' Gelfand pulled off the first one on a skate ramp somewhere in Florida. The ollie stayed a ramp-only trick for a few years. Then, in the early 1980s, legendary skater Rodney Mullen developed a flatland **version. Pretty soon the ollie had become one of the most important tricks in skating.**

If there's one thing that's important about learning to ollie a skateboard:
• **Bang the tail of the deck down HARD!**

FYI!

Don't try to ollie a longboard – they're so heavy it's practically impossible!

THE OLLIE

The ollie is the starting point for hundreds of modern skate tricks. If you can't do a smooth ollie without thinking about it, you won't be able to learn most of the tricks skaters perform. Here's how they are done:

3. The nose of the board will lift up and meet your front foot. This needs to be turned slightly inwards, so that the deck touches the outside edge of your shoe.

1. The ball of your back foot should be on the kicktail, and your front foot should be behind the front truck bolts. Now bend your knees way down (the lower you go, the higher the ollie will be).

2. Stand up, and bang the tail down on the ground as hard as you can. Just as it smacks the ground, jump both feet in the air, using your back foot to leap up. Jump with a quick, snappy movement.

flatland
skateboarding done on flat land, without ramps or obstacles of any kind

SECRET TRICK

When learning to ollie, you have a choice between learning standing still (for example on carpet or grass) or with the board rolling along.

It's easier to learn to ollie on a board that's rolling along slowly. Skaters who learn to ollie on a board that is standing still often pick up bad habits. They end up twisting slightly in the air, and when they do rolling ollies they find them hard to land well.

4. Roll your front foot over the front of the deck. This will level the board out in the air. The timing of this is tricky, and most people take weeks of practice to get it right. Don't worry if you spend a lot of time NOT doing an ollie!

5. Once you have the front-foot roll right, you'll be able to guide the board forward in the air and bring it up underneath your bent knees. As you return to earth your knees will straighten, but bend them as you land to absorb the shock.

Identifying **basic tricks**

Skateboarding tricks have hundreds of different names, and it's almost impossible to remember them all. To make things harder, tricks are done so fast that sometimes you'd have to rewind and watch them in slow motion to see what happened! Fortunately, this guide to basic trick names is here to help.

KICKTURNS

Kickturns are covered in more detail on page 37. In a kickturn, the rider puts his or her weight on the back of the board, lifting up the nose so that it is balanced on the back wheels. Then he or she swings the deck around to make a turn.

BOARD SLIDES

A board slide is when a skater ollies onto an obstacle such as a handrail, then slides along it on the underside of the deck. The obstacle is between the trucks, and the skater balances on either end of the board.

50/50 GRINDS

50/50 grinds are when a skater ollies up onto an obstacle, then **grinds** his or her trucks along it. If the skater grinds along balancing on just the rear truck, it is called a 5-0 grind (say 'five-OH', not 'five nothing' or 'five zero').

grind to slide along an obstacle on a skateboard's trucks
hard bail painful fall from a skateboard

ROCK 'N' ROLL

This trick is most often seen on a ramp or in a skate park. The skater rides up to the top of the ramp and lets the front truck go over the lip. Then he or she does a kickturn on the back trucks, drops back down the ramp and rides away. If the skater doesn't kickturn, but rides away fakie (backward), it's called a rock to fakie.

MANUALS

A manual is the skateboarding name for what most other sports call a wheelie. It is done by balancing on the back wheels while rolling along with the front wheels up in the air. A nose manual is the opposite, with the rear wheels up in the air. A manual is a deceptively tricky trick. It is easy to lose your balance and have the board shoot out ahead of or behind you. This almost always results in a **hard bail**.

KICKFLIPS

This is a trick most skaters learn as a progression from an ollie. While the board is in the air, the skater flicks it with his or her front foot to make it spin and flip over at least once. The kickflip is one of the many tricks developed by Rodney Mullen: it was originally called the magic flip, because it looked like magic!

FYI!

Rodney Mullen invented many of the tricks skaters use today, including the flatland ollie, kickflip, impossible, and the one-footed ollie. How many of those can you manage?

Ramp riding:
dropping in

Dropping in on a ramp is a mental challenge as much as a physical one. The first time you stand at the top and look down, the transition from being safe on the platform to hurtling downward looks pretty scary. Wearing pads and a helmet makes it feel a whole lot easier. And once you take a couple of falls you realize it's not that bad even if you *do* fall off.

The biggest lesson to learn about dropping in is:
• **Never hesitate. Once you've started, commit to the drop.**

coping
hard strip, usually metal, along the top edge of a skate ramp
double ramp
ramp made up of two slopes facing each other
quarterpipe
ramp made up of a single slope

BALANCE AT THE TOP OF THE RAMP
Rest the tail of your board flat on the **coping** at the edge of the ramp, keeping it in place with your back foot. The rest of the board, including both trucks and all the wheels, will be sticking out into space. When you feel balanced on your back foot, put your front foot on the deck over the front trucks. Keep all your weight on your back foot, though.

TAKE THE DROP
When you are ready to drop in, put your weight on your front foot and lean forward as the front of the board drops away. Crouch down and keep your knees bent. As the front wheel hits the ramp, commit your weight to both feet. If you hesitate at this point, you will fall backward and slide down the ramp in an undignified heap.

Skaters call smooth slopes in skate parks and elsewhere 'flow'. These tips will help you to ride over this kind of slope as smoothly as possible.

1 Always keep more weight on your front foot than your back foot. Don't tense up, though. You need to stay relaxed.

2 To keep speed and smoothness, bend your knees right up to absorb the up slopes, and let them extend a bit as you roll downward.

RIDE THROUGH

As you hit the bottom of the slope, use your knees to absorb the change of direction from 'down' to 'along'. Look up to see where you are headed. If you are learning to drop in, it might be best to find a ramp with a good run-off area, where you can lose speed without crashing into anything!

FYI!

It's best to learn to drop in on a small **quarterpipe** or similar ramp. Move to **double ramps** when you are more confident.

Simple and advanced transitions

Once you master the mental art of dropping in, it won't be long before you want to hit the double ramps. Start on a mini ramp like the one in the photos before graduating to a vert ramp. Of course, on a double-sided ramp, you drop in, then go up the ramp on the other side. Time to learn how to turn around, or 'transition'.

mini ramp small ramp, with non-vertical sides
nose manual riding a skateboard balancing on its two front wheels only
vert ramp large skate ramp with vertical side walls

If there's one thing you should remember about transitions:
• **Keep your knees bent at all times**

RIDE BACK FAKIE
The simplest transition is to ride back fakie. Drop in, then bend your knees to absorb the change from 'along' to 'up' as you hit the opposite ramp. When the skateboard slows down, turn your head and shoulders back in the direction you have come. Don't try to turn, just let the board roll back down the ramp. Keep your weight on the downhill foot with your knees bent, and you'll sucessfully ride out fakie.

KICKTURNS

In a kickturn, you balance the board momentarily on its back wheels and swing the front around so that the board turns through 180°. Use the basic ollie stance (see page 30). In the split second when the board slows to a stop on the opposite ramp, put about two-thirds of your weight on the tail, and twist your leading shoulder back the way you came. Your hips and feet will follow, turning the board around.

AERIALS

With enough speed to get above the top of the ramp, the best skaters are able to make their transitions in the air, spinning and twisting as they go. Tony Hawk, for example, amazed the skate world when he spun through 900° – two-and-a-half full turns – in 1999.

SECRET TRICK

Use nose stalls as a cool-looking transition on ramps:

1 As the board gets close to the top of the ramp, roll into a **nose manual**. Lean up toward the coping as you approach it.

2 Just before the front wheels ride off the top of the ramp, push down on your front foot so that the coping is caught between the nose and the front truck. Hang there looking cool for a split second, then drop back in.

Skateboard **etiquette**

Skating's good for you. It keeps you fit and improves your strength, reflexes and balance. But skateboarding can also be dangerous, so skaters have developed a set of guidelines for how to behave, whether you're in a skate park or out on the street.

! If you remember one thing about skate etiquette:
• **Always wear a helmet.**

RAMP RIDING ETIQUETTE
Because of the speeds, ramp riding can be especially dangerous. Expert skaters at any ramp expect each other to have good **etiquette**:
• Always wait your turn. Never **cut across** another skater.
• While waiting at the top of a ramp, stand back - get too close to the edge and you will interfere with whoever's riding.
• When you fall, get up and get out of the way as soon as you can.
• Give people a bit of encouragement if they pull off a new trick. Most people do this by whooping or banging the tail of their deck on the ground.

etiquette rules of acceptable and polite behavior

cut across ride in front of unexpectedly or aggressively

STREET SKATING ETIQUETTE

Nothing gets skating banned more quickly than complaints from non-skating members of the public. It's in everyone's interest to be polite and friendly at all times. On the street, always give pedestrians plenty of room. If you think you may have scared or annoyed someone, stop skating and apologize.

Longboarding
and **slalom**

Skateboarding isn't all about ramps and tricks. Some riders love the feeling of a longer board gliding its way across the concrete, like a snowboard in deep powder. A few have turned their love of longboarding into competition and take part in slalom or downhill races.

FYI!

Longboarding is similar to both surfing and snowboarding. Lots of surfers and snowboarders ride longboards for practice (as well as for fun).

For this kind of riding you need:
• **soft wheels, plus a longer deck that has plenty of flex**

PUMPING THE BOARD
In both longboarding and slalom, it's good to be able to **pump** the board up to a high speed. This allows you to put in more turns before you have to pump again. The technique is the same as on pages 26 and 27, but you have to bend your knees more – especially on the leg standing on the board. Take really long strides forward with your pumping leg, like someone stepping across a stream.

On a longboard, it's not always easy to know where to stand! Your basic stance is not as important as in standard skateboarding, but try this as a starting point:

1 Most people have a basic stance with their feet between the trucks, and a little more than shoulder-width apart.

2 Ride with your front foot at an angle of about 45°. Your back foot will probably feel most comfortable across the deck.

WORKING THE BOARD

Once you have speed, you want to keep it for as long as possible without having to pump again. You can do this by '**working**' the board. This is done using your front foot's grip on the deck of the board. As the board turns, swing your leading hip in the same direction to add power to the turn. When you turn the board the other way, do the same in reverse. (Notice that the more you bend your knees, the more speed you keep.)

pump to use your foot to push a skateboard forward
working adding speed using hip movements

41

Skateboarding **FAQs**

Almost all skaters sometimes have questions. Here are answers to some of the most frequently asked questions about skateboarding.

QUESTION 1: ARE CHEAP SKATEBOARDS OK?

It depends what you want from your board. If you plan to do a little bit of skating every now and then, a cheap board will be fine. But to get a board that will last through regular, hard use, you will have to pay more. (That doesn't mean all expensive boards are good quality, though – some are just expensive!)

QUESTION 2: HOW CAN I TELL IF A SKATEBOARD IS GOOD QUALITY?

Look at the wheels: only buy boards with urethane skate wheels, not plastic or rubber ones. Check that the bearings spin smoothly and freely. The trucks should be made of solid metal, and they shouldn't be painted over. You need a deck made of several layers of wood all glued together, with well-rounded, smoothed edges.

QUESTION 3: IS IT OK TO RIDE IN THE RAIN?

No. Water will work its way inside them, accompanied by tiny bits of grit and dirt, and wash out the lubricant. The bearings will soon be turning through a grinding soup of sludge and will have to be replaced.

QUESTION 4: IS IT A GOOD IDEA TO PRACTICE ON GRASS?

Practicing on grass (or carpet) can be helpful at the beginning when you are learning a new trick, but don't overdo it. After all, skateboarding tricks are done on wheels that roll, not wheels that won't move.

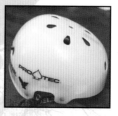

QUESTION 5: WHERE'S THE BEST PLACE TO BUY SKATE GEAR?

Buy your gear from a specialist store, where the staff are often skaters themselves. Employees can help you make decisions about what equipment is best for your style of skating and ability. Ideally, use a store that other skaters have recommended.

QUESTION 6: DO I NEED TO WEAR FLAT SHOES?

Yes. Flat shoes have the best grip on a deck. Also, there is no heel to get caught on the edges of the deck as you move.

SECRET TIP

If you find fear of falling is stopping you from learning new techniques, try these tricks to conquer your fear:

1 Practice with friends. It sounds silly, but with your friends encouraging you everything will seem easier.

2 Learn the difference between hurt (which quickly fades away) and damaged (which can take a long time to repair). You *will* hurt yourself skating. Get up, take a breather, and then get on with it.

Technical skateboard
language

7-ply wood made out of seven thin layers glued together

ABEC measuring system showing the quality of ball bearings

bearing shield plastic or rubber cover that shields bearings from water and dirt

bradawl tool with a thin, pointed tip, which is used to make holes

concave amount of lift in the nose, tail and sides of a skateboard deck

coping hard strip, usually of metal, along the top edge of a skate ramp

cut across ride in front of unexpectedly or aggressively

double ramp ramp made up of two slopes facing each other

durometer rating number showing how hard a skateboard wheel is

etiquette rules of acceptable and polite behavior

fakie traveling backward on a skateboard

flatland skateboarding done on flat land, without ramps or obstacles of any kind

goofy foot right-foot-forward

grind to slide along an obstacle on a skateboard's trucks

hallmarked mark showing that goods meet safety standards

hanger wide part of a truck, on to which the wheels are bolted

hard bail painful fall from a skateboard

heel side edge of a skateboard deck to which the skater's heels are closest

manual trick where the skater rides along balancing on only the back wheels

mini ramp small skate ramp, with non-vertical sides

nose manual when a skateboard rides on its two front wheels only

ollie when a skater jumps the board into the air using only his/her feet

Phillips head screwdriver tip or screw with a narrow, four-pointed-star shape

pump to use your foot to push a skateboard forward

quarterpipe ramp made up of a single slope

socket wrench type of wrench that fits over a nut and is used to undo it

spacer piece of plastic fitted between skateboard trucks and the deck

spacers pieces of plastic used inside skateboard wheels to keep bearings the correct distance apart

stance how a skater stands on the board

toe side edge of a skateboard deck to which the skater's toes are closest

vert ramp large skate ramp with vertical side walls

washer tiny metal ring that fits either side of a skateboard wheel

X Games extreme sports competition featuring many skateboarding events

Further information

REFERENCE BOOKS

There are lots of beginner's books about skateboarding, but not as many aimed at more advanced riders. These are some of the best:

Skateboarding Skills: The Rider's Guide
Ben Powell (Firefly Books, 2008)

Written by the editor of *Sidewalk Surfer* magazine, this book has plenty of basic information on skateboarding, from board set-up to techniques and tricks.

Skateboarding: New Levels – Tips and Tricks for Serious Riders
Doug Werner and Steve Badillo (Tracks Publishing, 2002)

This book reviews the basics and includes sections about building your own ramp and interviews with pro riders. The main focus is on showing intermediate skaters how to improve their range of tricks and skills.

Skateboarding is Not a Crime James Davis and Skin Philips (Carlton Books, 2004)

This book features excellent photos, showing the development of skateboarding from the 1950s onwards. Davis is a columnist for *Sidewalk Surfer*, and contributor to *Transworld Skateboarding*, and Skin Philips is a well-known skate photographer.

WEBSITES

FactHound offers a safe, fun way to find Internet sites related to this book. All of the sites on FactHound have been researched by our staff.

Here's all you do:

Visit **www.facthound.com**

Type in this code: 9781429668835

Skate timeline

1950s
The decade in which skateboarding is invented in California by surfers practicing on dry land. No one knows the exact year, or who was the first skater (but there are plenty of people who *claim* it was them).

1960 onwards
Skateboarding's popularity grows massively, as non-surfers start skating. Freestyle skateboarding appears. These choreographed routines feature flatland tricks, which are set to music in the same way as figure skating.

1963
Skateboarding reaches its first peak of popularity. There are now dedicated skateboard brands and lots of competitions. But in the next couple of years, skateboarding suddenly becomes far less popular, leading many people to think that skating has disappeared forever.

1966 onwards
People do carry on skateboarding, but far fewer of them. Skateboard companies start to go out of business, leading to skaters hoarding gear or making their own equipment.

1972
A massive landmark in skateboarding, as Frank Nasworthy invents modern urethane skateboard wheels. The wheels are so good to skate on that they spark a whole new interest in skating.

1975
The Zephyr skate team blows away crowds at The Ocean Festival in Del Mar, California. Their aggressive, inventive style of skateboarding was a revolution in skateboarding, and made riders such as Tony Alva, Jay Adams and Stacy Peralta world famous.

1976-1978
Alan Gelfand develops the ollie, modern skateboarding's key trick (sources differ as to exactly when he first performed the trick).

1979
A big increase in the cost of insuring skate parks against injuries forces many to close. Skateboarding's popularity suddenly crashes.

1980s
Skateboarding goes underground, with fewer people skating. The sport is no longer big business, and most skate companies are owned by skaters. As a result, skateboarding becomes increasingly creative and radical in its equipment and techniques.

1984
Stacey Peralta and George Powell make the first skateboarding video: *Bones Brigade Video Show*. It is soon followed by more videos, which allow skaters to see what other people around the world are doing, spot new tricks, and feel part of a bigger community of skaters.

North America's Dew Tour contest begins in 2005, and quickly rivals the X Games. Everything from small local contests to big international events start to appear. Skateboarding has hit the mainstream.

2001

The documentary *Dogtown and Z-Boys* comes out. It tells the story of the revolutionary Zephyr skate team of the late 1970s. The documentary is successful far beyond a skating audience, and leads a lot of old skaters to root around in the garage and unearth their old decks.

2002

Tony Hawk Pro Skater 1 comes out for Nintendo 64, and is a huge hit. It is the first of many Tony Hawk computer games, every one of them a success. The popularity of the games feeds into real-life skating.

2004

The International Skateboarding Federation is founded, partly with the aim of getting skateboarding into the Olympics.

1988 onwards

Skateboarding dives in popularity yet again. Most skaters are interested in street skating, and the pro vert scene hits tough times.

1989

The movie *Gleaming the Cube* comes out, with Christian Slater playing its skateboarding teenage hero. Famous skaters such as Tony Hawk appear in the film, and suddenly increasing numbers of people start getting into skating again.

1990s

Street skating becomes more popular, but this time skateboarding is associated with a punky, grungy image.

1995

The Extreme Games contest is held in Rhode Island. The Games feature skateboarding competitions, and bring new attention to the sport. The next year, this competition was renamed the X Games. As a result of the X Games, skateboarding starts to be called an 'extreme sport.' Not all skaters are happy with this description, or the way their underground activity is becoming mainstream.

2000 onwards

Skateboarding contests and competitions become increasingly popular, driven partly by the demand for skating on TV.

Index